SPORTS FROM COAST TO COAST™

PAINTBALL
RULES, TIPS, STRATEGY, AND SAFETY

GREG ROZA

rosen publishing's
rosen central®

New York

To Greg, Lisl, and Frankenfish

Published in 2007 by The Rosen Publishing Group, Inc.
29 East 21st Street, New York, NY 10010

First Edition

Library of Congress Cataloging-in-Publication Data

Roza, Greg.
Paintball: rules, tips, strategy, and safety/Greg Roza.—1st ed.
    p. cm.—(Sports from coast to coast)
Includes bibliographical references and index.
ISBN-13: 978-1-4042-0994-7
ISBN-10: 1-4042-0994-8 (library binding)
1. Paintball (Game)—Juvenile literature. I. Title. II. Series.
GV1202.S87R69 2007
796.2—dc22

                                   2006009998

Manufactured in the United States of America

CONTENTS

CHAPTER ONE

The History of Paintball

The sport of paintball was still in its infancy when this player was photographed competing in the early 1980s. Notice that players in the early years did not wear a lot of protective gear.

You are crouched behind a fallen tree, scanning the area ahead of you. Occasionally, you glance behind. A gentle breeze blows through the branches above you. Your heart is still racing from the sprint through the woods, along the creek, and up the hill to your current position. You check yourself for paint splatter, but you are clean. As you try to plan your next move, you hear a twig snap nearby. Silently, motionlessly, you stay low and glance about. You know you have to move soon or you will be trapped.

Suddenly, a paintball explodes on the fallen tree right next to you! Wheeling around, you see two people in masks closing in on you. You hurdle the tree as more paintballs splat around you. The chase is on again. Your survival instincts tell you to duck behind the next tree and prepare to return fire. As you slide to a stop, a paintball explodes dangerously close to your leg, but you made it to cover. You quickly peek out and fire paintballs rapidly, catching one of your opponents squarely in the chest. "Out!" he yells. But you have little time to gloat, as a paintball splatters across your mask. "Out!" you yell reluctantly.

You and your opponent leave the playing field together, laughing and talking about the chase through the woods. Hearts pounding and breathing rapidly, both of you are already looking forward to the next match. Next time, you think, I will survive and win . . .

What Is Paintball?

Paintball is still a relatively new sport that offers participants many exciting ways to play. All of the different games involve "marking" other players with small, paint-filled capsules shot out of paintball "markers," or guns. The paintballs explode on impact, leaving a splotch of bright paint on a player's clothes. A player who has been "marked," or hit by a paintball, is out of the game until the next round begins.

The markers used in paintball were originally developed in the early 1970s by an American company, Daisy Manufacturing. This is the same company that invented the BB gun in 1886. The first paintball markers were not intended for sport. Rather, they were designed for use in the forestry and cattle industries. Forestry workers used them to mark trees that were to be removed. Cattle workers used them to mark individual animals that were to be separated from the herd.

The Birth of Survival

In the late 1970s, two friends from New Hampshire—writer and hunter Charles Gaines and Wall Street stockbroker Hayes Noel—frequently discussed human survival instincts. They had differing views on what it takes to survive when placed in a desperate situation and they were both eager to test their survival skills in such a situation. They tried to come up with different ways to safely "hunt" each other in a natural setting, but they never developed a concrete plan. A few times they "hunted" each other through the woods with tomatoes!

In the early 1980s, Gaines and Noel found a better way to evaluate their survivalist instincts. While reading an agricultural magazine, they discovered paint markers that were designed to stain trees that had to be cut down. Instantly, the two men knew they had stumbled upon something big. They ordered two of the markers and tested them, discovering that they were powerful and accurate enough to use in a mock hunting situation. Equally important, they did not do serious damage to people. It wasn't long before they used the markers in a duel; Noel missed, but Gaines—the experienced hunter—hit his prey. After this short experiment, they began to push the boundaries of their survivalist instincts by stalking each other through the woods, each trying to mark the other before being marked himself. This was the birth of a game they called Survival.

With the aid of sporting goods dealer Bob Gurnsey, Gaines and Noel developed the rules for a large-group version of Survival. In June 1981, Gurnsey, Gaines, and Noel, plus nine other men from all over the country, gathered in an eighty-acre area of woods in New Hampshire to play the new game. They each had a paintball marker, a pair of shop goggles, and a map of the area. Within the playing field were a referee and four stations set up with flags. The object of the game was to collect one flag from each station and return with the flags to the player's home base without being marked by another player. Any player who was hit with a paintball was eliminated from the game. During the two-and-a-half-hour competition,

The Nel-Spot 007

Paintball markers were around for about a decade before the first paintball game was played. The first mass-marketed paintball marker was the Nel-Spot 007 *(right)*, which was developed by the Daisy Manufacturing Co. for the Nelson Paint Company. Instead of shooting rounds, the Nel-Spot 007 fires specially designed paintballs, which are loaded into a magazine above the barrel.

Measuring eleven inches long and weighing about three pounds empty, the Nel-Spot 007 is powered by a 12-gram CO_2 cartridge, which is stored in the grip. Each cartridge can fire twenty to thirty paintballs before needing to be replaced.

Because it is reliable and accurate, the Nel-Spot 007 became the marker of choice for early paintball players. In fact, it was the type of marker used by all twelve players during the first paintball game, in 1981. For its importance in paintball history, the Nel-Spot 007 became famous in its own right. Thousands of paintball players continued to use the 007 into the 1990s, even as more advanced paintball markers were introduced.

ten of the twelve players were eliminated from play. The winner of the game, local lumberjack and deer hunter Richard White, never even fired a paintball!

Paintball Explodes!

One of the men invited to the first game of Survival was Bob Jones, a writer for *Sports Illustrated*, a popular sports magazine. He was given permission to write an article about the event. Gurnsey, Gaines, and Noel realized they had invented something that a lot of people were going to go crazy for once they read about it. They decided to call the young sport National Survival Game (NSG), which was also the name they gave their new company. Through NSG, they helped others set up paintball fields, and they made money by selling paintball markers and equipment. Initially, NSG made a considerable profit distributing paintball gear. However, once the word about paintball got out, it wasn't long before paintball franchises began springing up across the northeastern United States.

In 1982, two paintball fanatics from Chicago, Jeff Perlmutter and David Freeman, founded a company called Pursuit Marketing, Inc. (PMI). After unsuccessfully trying to work with NSG, Perlmutter and Freeman decided that they could market paintball themselves. Soon, people all over the country were ordering supplies from PMI. Most orders were from those who wanted to start their own Survival companies, and they often ordered thirty markers at a time. Interest in Survival exploded in the United States. Within a few years, NSG and PMI were not the only companies offering gear for this exciting new game.

Many newcomers to the sport did not want to spend hours wandering around eighty acres of woods. They wanted a quicker game with more action. As paintball became more popular, it transformed into a team sport different from the one-against-all competition that Noel and Gaines had invented.

In April 1982, Caleb Strong opened the first outdoor paintball field, in Rochester, New York. Other cities, including London, Ontario, soon had their own outdoor fields, too. The first National Survival Game Championship took place in 1983, in Grantham, New Hampshire. The first-prize winners—the Unknown Rebels from London, Ontario—walked away with $3,000! In November 1984, Strong opened the first indoor paintball facility, in Buffalo, New York. Similar facilities began opening up in England, France, Germany, Spain, and Australia. Interest in paintball had erupted like a wildfire and spread to countries all over North America, South America, Europe, and Asia,

In 1984, paintball pioneer Caleb Strong opened the first indoor paintball facility, in Buffalo, New York. The facility quickly became popular. On April 22, 1986, *The Buffalo News* (*facing page*) profiled the indoor game, which locals called Splatball.

The dark, eerie atmosphere is all part of the team game of make-believe combat called Indoor Splatball.

RICHARD W. ROELLER/Buffalo News

S·P·L·A·T·B·A·L·L!

Combat Game Comes Indoors

By ANTHONY VIOLANTI

Someone tried to tell her, but she didn't seem to understand. There was a time when instead of shooting people, college students were handing out flowers and making peace signs. Lynette Rhodes looked up, smiled and calmly loaded her gun.

Don't worry, it's only a game. Maybe it's a sign of the times, but on a recent spring morning, in an old, chilly, damp, dark building — an annex of the Buffalo Tennis and Racquetball Center on Elmwood Avenue — about 25 Buffalo State College students gathered for a session of something called Indoor Splatball.

This is a weird sort of game. Thirty players divided into two teams are each armed with carbon dioxide-powered guns that shoot gelatin-filled balls that "splat" upon impact. Once you have been splatted, you are out of the game.

The object of the game is to capture the other team's flag on the other side of the building. While doing that, team members splat as many opponents as possible. The moral here is: splat onto others before they splat onto you.

Hey, wait a minute. This might be dangerous. Suppose somebody enjoys splatting so much that he or she decides to make like Dirty Harry or Charles Bronson and goes out on the streets and starts picking off real people with real bullets.

"That kind of criticism is just a bunch of liberal garbage," Martin Crawford, a 23-year-old paramedic, assures a visitor. Crawford, a firearms enthusiast, started playing indoor splatball a few weeks ago and already is devoted to the pastime.

"It's just a game," Crawford says. "It's like being a kid again, playing cops and robbers. I don't intend to play this and then go out on the streets and start blowing people away."

Lynette Rhodes also enjoys the game. Before it was about to begin, someone asks what brought her out on a Saturday for this shoot-'em-up. Ms. Rhodes, 22, an education major at Buffalo State, is taking her first excursion into the world of splatball.

Indoor splatball is growing in popularity among women. About 25 percent of the players (who must be at

See Splatball
Page C-2, Column 1

Splatball players listen attentively as Mark Gilbride gives instructions, far left; two players discuss strategy over a map of the building, center; and Lynette Rhodes loads her splat gun, right.

and in South Africa. Initially a male-only sport, paintball is now enjoyed by many women, too. Today, about 15 percent of paintball players are women.

Is It Violent?

It should come as no surprise that many people have objected to paintball, labeling it a violent game that simulates warfare and glamorizes guns. However, despite some similarities with military and law enforcement tactics, the sport is not especially violent. The attraction for many dedicated players is the opportunity to demonstrate superior survival skills.

According to Noel, paintball received unfair negative publicity in the early years due to its military look. The guns, camouflage, and goggles presented a violent image to those who were seeing the sport for the first time. It was hard for Noel and Gaines to make some people understand that violence was not what paintball was all about. To them, and to the majority of the sport's die-hard fans, paintball is about sportsmanship, creativity, fun, and being a team player. Most of all, the sport of paintball is about the desire to compete and survive under difficult and rapidly changing conditions.

Going Pro

Most paintball players enjoy the sport as a weekend pastime. Some, however, have turned this weekend hobby into a professional activity. The first professional paintball league, the International Paintball Players Association (IPPA), was established in 1988. The IPPA disbanded in 1996. Today, there are many pro and semipro leagues in the United States and Canada. The most notable of these leagues is the National Professional Paintball League (NPPL),

This flyer *(facing page)* advertised the third annual North American Survival Game Championship, held in 1985. The winner received a trophy named for Mack Bolan, a well-known character in action-adventure novels.

The military look of early Survival is evident in this team photo of the Unknown Rebels of London, Ontario. They won the first National Survivor Game Championship, held in 1983.

which was established in 1992, and the National X Ball League (NXL), which was founded in 2002. Pro teams are often sponsored by companies that make and sell paintball equipment.

In addition to pro leagues, there is a college league, the National Collegiate Paintball Association (NCPA). Playing for a college paintball team can prepare you for playing professional paintball.

Pros earn money from sponsorships and endorsements, and some earn prize money for winning big tournaments. A few big-name paintball players have made money by starting their own paintball companies.

While most professional paintball players do not make much money, or any money at all, this could change as the sport grows in popularity. In early 2006, paintball superstar Oliver Lang accepted a $100,000 offer to leave the San Diego Dynasty to play for a team called the Ironmen, founded by the paintball retailer DYE Precision, Inc. This is the most endorsement money any paintball player has ever received. Many players think this development could be the beginning of paintball as a high-paying sport.

CHAPTER TWO

Equipment and Clothing

These professional paintball players have top-of-the-line markers, masks, equipment, and uniforms. Beginners don't need this level of equipment when learning how to play.

To equip yourself properly, you can expect to spend between $100 and $200 on new equipment for your first paintball match. However, you can usually rent equipment for less. Some sporting goods stores and online shops offer starter kits that cost between $80 and $100.

Equipment

Starter kits usually contain a marker, a hopper, one or two compressed air cartridges, goggles, a mask, and paintballs. More experienced players and tournament participants may want to purchase gloves, ankle protectors, uniforms, pricier markers, and other accessories.

Markers

Paintball markers, also called paintball guns, launch paintballs using compressed air. Although there are several different systems, all markers work the same way. First, the marker must be cocked. This means the bolt is slid back so that a paintball falls into the barrel. When the trigger is pulled, a burst of air from an air tank forces the paintball out of the marker through the open end of the barrel. The process is repeated every time a paintball is fired. There are several marker styles and brands, so you may want to try different kinds until you find the one you like best. There are three main types of firing systems used in paintball markers:

- **Pump-action.** This is the simplest type of marker, perfect for beginners. Pump-action—or stock—markers need to be cocked every time you want to fire a paintball. They generally require small air tanks that can fire between fifteen and twenty-five paintballs before a new tank is needed.
- **Semiautomatic.** The most commonly used type of firing system, semiautomatic markers need to be cocked only once, manually. After this, every time the trigger is pulled, the marker automatically slides the bolt back and loads a new paintball into the barrel, allowing for faster shooting. Some semiautomatic markers use compressed air to complete this process, while others use an electric motor.
- **Fully automatic.** This style of marker continues to fire paintballs as long as the trigger is held down. Many tournaments and leagues ban fully automatic markers because they give an unfair advantage over players using semiautomatic markers.

Air Tanks

Markers require a propellant, or compressed gas, to launch paintballs. The traditional option for compressed air is carbon dioxide (CO_2). Compressed nitrogen (NO_2) and high-pressure air (HPA) also have become popular forms of propellant, although they are more expensive than CO_2. Propellant comes in a small aluminum cartridge that screws directly onto the marker. Air tanks attach differently to paintball markers depending on their design. Some screw into the back end of the marker, and some attach to the bottom. Others attach beneath and parallel to the marker's barrel. The smallest tanks hold twelve grams of compressed air, last for about fifteen to twenty-five shots, and are disposable. Larger tanks can be refilled. The largest tanks hold twenty ounces of air and can fire more than 1,000 paintballs before needing to be refilled.

To avoid switching air tanks in the middle of a competition, some players prefer to use a remote air supply. Remotes are large air tanks that are carried in a backpack, rather than screwed directly into the marker. They are linked to the marker via a long, flexible tube. Remote tanks make the marker itself lighter and easier to handle. Some players, however, complain that the flexible tubes get snagged on branches or other obstructions.

Paintballs

During a typical thirty-minute round of paintball, a player may fire dozens—perhaps hundreds—of paintballs. A paintball is a round capsule filled with paint, also called marking dye. Paintballs range from 0.50 inches (1.3 centimeters) to 0.72 inches (1.8 cm), but the most common size is 0.68 inches

The top image (*facing page*) shows a young competitor holding a semiautomatic paintball marker, with hopper and air tank attached. This type of marker is popular and relatively affordable. The diagram at bottom identifies the various parts of a typical semiautomatic paintball marker.

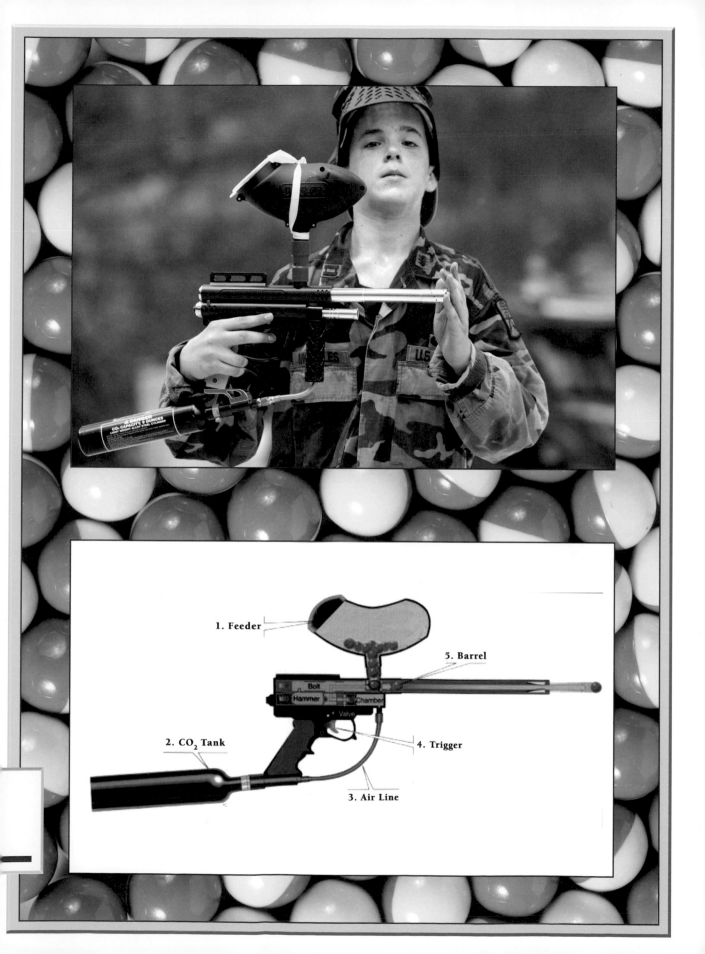

1. Feeder

5. Barrel

Bolt

Hammer

Chamber

Valve

2. CO$_2$ Tank

4. Trigger

3. Air Line

(1.7 cm). Each paintball weighs only a few grams. (A penny weighs about three grams.) The paint inside the ball is non-toxic, biodegradable, and water-soluble. It comes in a variety of bright colors, which helps in determining which player or team made a hit during a game.

The outer covering of the paintball capsule is made of gelatin. This capsule is strong enough so that it does not rupture when being handled, but it is weak enough to break upon impact when fired from a marker. Upon bursting, the paintball leaves a mark that is about six inches (15.2 cm) in diameter. The farther a paintball travels, the slower it moves, and the greater the chance that it will not break on impact. Players should not try to reuse paintballs that don't break. The capsule may have been weakened, so the paintball has a greater chance of exploding while inside the barrel of the marker.

The player in this photo is wearing a belt pack, or harness, designed specifically for paintball. This accessory allows a player easy access to extra air tanks and paintball containers.

Hoppers

A hopper is a storage container for paintballs. It is like an upside-down bottle that connects directly to the top of a marker and feeds paintballs into the marker one at a time. Standard hoppers use gravity to load paintballs into the marker. When a paintball is fired and the marker is empty, another paintball falls into place. Then the marker is ready to be fired again. Most hoppers on the market today hold 200 paintballs.

Some players use motorized hoppers, which load the marker quicker than gravity. Agitating hoppers have rotating parts that make the paintballs fall, rather than relying on gravity to do the work. Force-feed hoppers use a spring or another method to force the paintball into the marker. Motorized hoppers are quicker than gravity hoppers, but they also jam more frequently.

Squeegees

On occasion, a paintball may explode while inside the barrel of a marker. This usually makes the marker unusable. For this reason, most paintball players carry squeegees with them onto the field. A squeegee is a long rod with a sponge or cloth attached to the end. It is thin enough to be inserted into the barrel. The sponge or cloth cleans paint from the inside of the barrel so that it can be used again.

Clothes and Safety Gear

Thick, protective clothing is a must when playing paintball. While it is generally considered a very safe sport, paintball does involve projectiles that can travel up to 300 feet (91.4 meters) per second. These projectiles are not capable of piercing clothing. They can, however, cause a stinging sensation and even leave

Safety clothing is essential. This player is wearing a mask and goggles, padded uniform, gloves, and leg protectors. Only his fingers are exposed.

bruises. Because of these potential dangers, protective clothing is absolutely necessary. Most players wear long shirts, long pants, goggles, helmets, masks, and gloves.

Protecting Your Head

Goggles and face masks are the most important pieces of equipment when playing paintball. A flying paintball can seriously injure unprotected eyes and ears. Players are not allowed anywhere near the playing field without goggles and a face mask. Removing goggles during a game results in an instant ejection from the match. It is important to wear regulation paintball goggles, rather than ski goggles, lab goggles, or any other non-regulation eyewear. Regulation goggles can withstand being hit with a paintball traveling 400 feet (122 m) per second, fired from 3 feet (approximately 1 m) away.

This paintball player wears a protective mask and goggles. The mask is well ventilated, allowing him to breathe easily during a heated competition.

Paintball Clothing

The type of shoes you wear depends on the terrain of the playing field. When playing on a grass or dirt field or on artificial turf, sneakers are usually best. Many players prefer to wear sports cleats for better traction. Boots are best when playing in a wooded area that may contain creeks, hills, and gullies. In general, the lighter the shoe, the more comfortable you'll be.

Paintball Markers and the Law

The federal government does not regulate paintball markers as it does actual firearms (guns). However, federal law does say that the use of a "look-alike" firearm in any criminal activity will result in the same penalties as if an actual firearm was used. It's also against federal law to board an airplane with containers of compressed air. If you must fly with your paintball equipment, never bring compressed air with you. Notify the airline before arriving at the airport, and secure all equipment in luggage that can be checked before getting on the plane.

You should always be aware of local laws regarding paintball markers and equipment. Local governments often have specific laws regarding their use, and some laws are stricter than others. You should also keep in mind that a paintball marker looks very much like a real firearm—especially with the hopper and air tanks removed. Carrying it in public places, such as a park or playground, is asking for trouble. Police officers may think you are carrying a real gun, and they would be justified in taking the steps necessary to detain you. Always transport your paintball marker in an appropriate case or bag.

Uniforms and/or colored armbands are mandatory during regulation tournaments. Some players choose to wear camouflage, especially during games that take place in a wooded area. This is not necessary, but it does provide an edge. Players wearing camouflage blend into their surroundings better, increasing their chances of surviving the game.

Many experienced players choose to wear harnesses when playing paintball. A harness is an article of clothing that contains tight straps or loops designed to hold air cartridges, paintball containers, a squeegee, and sometimes a second marker. Some harnesses are slung over the shoulder or around the neck, others are worn like a belt, and the rest are secured tightly to arms and legs.

CHAPTER THREE

The Rules of Paintball

There are dozens of different paintball games that are popular today, so specific rules depend on the variation you are playing. However, there are some rules common to all paintball games.

Common Rules

The number-one rule of paintball is to keep your goggles on at all times. Being struck in the eye with a paintball can cause serious injuries, even blindness. Sometimes, in the heat of a competition, goggles can become foggy, reducing a player's vision. Still, this is no reason to remove them. Any player caught without regulation protective eyewear in the "goggle zone" is immediately ejected from the competition.

Physical contact is not allowed during paintball. In fact, a player should not be within five feet (1.5 m) of a player from another team. This

Taking a "head-shot" is not that uncommon in today's fast-paced paintball competitions. This player is smart to be playing by the rules, with full eye protection and facemask in place.

rule is designed to prevent players from being hurt by paintballs fired at close range. When two opponents come within five feet of each other, one or both must move back before firing. Failing to do so will result in one or both players being ejected from the game.

When a paintball breaks on your uniform, gear, or marker, even if it was fired by a teammate, you must immediately raise your arms, loudly declare "out" or "hit," and use the safest and shortest route to leave the field. This lets others know that you are out of the current match. If two players mark each other at the same time, both must leave the field. If you are struck by a paintball that does not break, you may continue playing. Once you call yourself out, it is against the rules for others to keep firing at you.

If you are unsure whether you have been hit, ask for a paint check. Opponents may not try to mark you while you are being paint-checked. If the referee sees that you have been marked, he or she will call you out. (Usually the mark must be at least the size of a U.S. quarter.) If you have not been marked, the referee will announce that you are still in the game. When you declare yourself out, you must leave the field whether you were hit or not. So, when in doubt, don't call yourself out until you get a paint check.

Common Tactics

While different variations of paintball require specific strategies, there are general tactics that every player should understand in order to play the best game possible. One of the most important tactics of paintball is to keep moving. Rule number one is not to sit in the same spot for too long. Staying

No Game for Cheaters

All regulation paintball competitions feature at least one referee to make sure everyone plays fairly. However, referees cannot be everywhere and see everything that occurs during a match, especially on large outdoor fields. This gives dishonest players opportunities to cheat. Some may try to wipe paint off of their uniforms after being hit. Others may set their markers to fire paintballs faster or more frequently than regulations allow. Most serious paintball players pride themselves on

A referee checks a player's uniform for paint during a competition. Tournament referees go through training to learn safety, positioning, rules, and making the right call under pressure.

playing fairly. To them, if you can't win while playing by the rules, you don't have what it takes to be a paintball survivalist. Being a good paintball player means respecting other players and playing fair.

stationary allows other players to sneak up on you. Besides, most variations of paintball require a team or player to achieve an objective, such as capturing a flag. You can't do this by sitting in one place the entire game.

If you are unsuccessful at hitting a player who is hiding behind a wall or bunker, do not keep firing paintballs from your current position. Instead, think creatively and quickly. Changing position may give you a new view of your opponents, and it will keep them guessing what you will do next.

Sometimes it is necessary to rush at another player who has "bunkered down" behind an obstruction. This is a dangerous move because it puts you out in the open. However, by rushing forward, you often create a diversion for

The player on the right boldly snuck up on his opponent. The player on his knees behind the bunker thought he was safe, but he failed to watch his back. *Splat!* He never saw it coming.

other players on your team. This allows them to move forward and possibly take out the opponent. In general, it is the aggressive players who excel in the sport of paintball.

Just as it is important to keep your body moving, it is also important to keep your eyes moving. Never focus on just one target or area of the playing field. When moving forward, don't forget to look left and right—and even behind you. By remaining alert, you increase your chances of staying in the game.

Boundaries

Referee

Bunker

Referee

Flag Station

Flag Station

Referee

Bunker

Players
Eliminated
From Game

Above all, remember that paintball is a game of survival. The better players are creative in finding ways to win, even when stuck in tough situations. For example, if you run out of paintballs, don't give up. You can continue to be of value to your team by drawing fire away from teammates who still have plenty of paintballs to finish the game.

Paintball Variations

When Noel and Gaines first envisioned paintball, they pictured a one-against-all type of survival game. Once paintball caught on, however, team play became more popular. Today, people play numerous game variations. Listed in this section are just a few of the more popular ones.

Capture the Flag

Capture the flag is usually played by two teams on a medium- to large-size field with a variety of natural or man-made obstructions. Each team has a base and a flag. The winner is the team that steals the other's flag and returns it to their home base without being marked.

During capture the flag, both teams have defensive and offensive players. The offensive players quickly move out and try to take the other team's flag. The defensive players protect their own flag from being swiped. Team captains organize their players and give orders.

In a variation of capture the flag called center-flag, both teams must try to steal the same flag. As the name suggests, the center-flag is positioned in the center of the field. The first team to return the flag to their base is the winner.

The player in the top image (*opposite page*) has successfully captured the opposing team's flag. He still needs to make it back to his team's base without getting marked. The bottom diagram demonstrates a typical setup for capture the flag.

Players of the National Professional Paintball League (NPPL) begin a capture the flag competition. The teams enter at opposite ends of a 180-foot (54.86 m) long, 100-foot (30.48 m) wide field covered with inflatable bunkers.

Total Elimination

The object of the game total elimination is to remove opposing players from the match by marking them with a paintball. This variation is usually played on a small- or medium-size field with man-made obstructions. Total elimination is usually played with two teams, but it can also be played with a one-against-all format. Some players call this variation speedball because it is a fast-paced game.

Whether the game is capture the flag, total elimination, or some other variation, a player who is marked is eliminated from the game. After being marked, this player properly raises his hands to signal to other players that he has been hit and is leaving the playing area.

Scenario

Scenario games are matches that follow a given set of circumstances, or a scenario. These are usually held on medium or large outdoor fields. Some groups meet to reenact historic battles. Others play through generic situations, like in a variation called supply chain. During this scenario, one team has to transport cargo (for instance, three portable coolers filled with fake supplies) from one point to another, while the other team attempts to steal that cargo.

Scenario matches often last from six to eight hours, and some last for a full twenty-four hours. Some scenario gatherings are attended by hundreds of players and often end in a dramatic battle.

X Ball

In X ball, two teams of five race to swipe a flag placed at the center of the field. A team is awarded a point for "hanging the flag" in their base. Once a team hangs the flag, they are awarded a point, and both teams take a three-minute timeout. When the next round begins, five players from each team return to the field. They can be the same five who were on the field for the previous round, or they can be new players. The team that hangs the flag the most during two twenty-minute halves is declared the winner. Similar to hockey, players who break the rules in X ball must sit in a penalty box for a few minutes before rejoining play.

Who's Who

The types of paintball players vary depending on the kind of game being played. Sometimes players are referred to by the position they take on the field, such as front middle or back left. In flag games, the person with the flag is called the flag runner. Or you may refer to players based on their job, such as defense or offense.

A sniper is a player who takes up a hidden position and tries to hit opponents without being seen. Snipers are helpful when the element of surprise is a must. They are perfect for defending a base against unsuspecting attackers.

Some players excel at bunkering. At the beginning of most paintball matches, it is essential to rush forward and control as much of the field as possible by hiding behind an obstruction or bunker and marking anyone who comes out into the open. To take out someone who is controlling a bunker, you must rush forward and put yourself at risk. However, allowing an opponent to bunker unchallenged can cost you the game.

This sniper crouches behind a stack of wood during a paintball match, defending her team's flag. To be effective, snipers must be silent . . . and patient.

Every team has a captain. Captains speak with the referees before and after the game to receive information and scores. They help keep a team organized and focused on the mission. College and pro teams also have coaches. Coaches usually aren't players, but they can yell information to players during a game.

CHAPTER FOUR

Getting Involved

Even though he is not wearing a flashy, expensive uniform, this young player has everything he needs to join a paintball match.

It is not difficult to break into the sport of paintball. The first step is to purchase the necessary equipment. Paintball gear can be bought at large sporting goods stores, at smaller shops that specialize in paintball equipment, and from online distributors. Once you have your equipment, you need to learn how to use and care for it properly. Most store and field owners will show you how to use, maintain, and protect your gear. Habitual players often prefer to have their own equipment. But if you are just starting out, many fields will supply you with everything you need for an afternoon of paintball. A trial run may help you decide if you like the sport.

Once you have the gear, you need somewhere to play. Many cities in the United States now have one or more paintball facilities in or just outside of the city limits. Larger outdoor fields can also be found in more secluded areas, miles away from cities. Both indoor and outdoor arenas continue to spring up all over the country, most of them featuring their own paintball shops. Fields usually charge about $30 per person and require that you use paintballs purchased from their shop. While private fields usually don't have age restrictions, insured fields do, based on local laws.

Next, it's time to find others who share your interest in paintball. Often this is as easy as convincing three or four friends to purchase or rent the necessary equipment and join you. There are also hundreds of local paintball associations and Internet forums for people interested in the sport. These resources help players meet and plan competitions and get-togethers. Some groups of friends prefer to stage their own paintball outings in forests or fields on private property. Keep in mind, however, that you should still follow the same rules and safety guidelines that regulation fields enforce to avoid arguments and injuries.

Each time you play paintball, you will improve your skills and tactics. You will get better at bunkering, charging your opponent, and avoiding paintballs fired by other players. Experienced players like to be creative and are always looking for new ways to outsmart their opponents.

Play It Safe

Paintball is often labeled a violent activity that involves harming others. This simply isn't true. Physical contact between players is strictly forbidden. As with all organized sports, paintball is just a game and isn't worth fighting

This photo shows why experienced paintball players wear gloves during competitions. When a paintball hits exposed skin, it can leave a nasty welt.

over. When you follow the rules and prepare for your own safety and the safety of others, paintball is an exciting, harmless, and friendly activity.

Dress the Part

Paintballs can bruise and even break bare skin when they're fired at a very close range. This is why regulation play requires players to be at least five feet (1.5 m) apart. At this distance, a hit may sting (depending on the amount of protective clothing you are wearing) but should not bruise or break the skin.

While being hit with a paintball can hurt, protective clothing will prevent any real harm. The clothes you wear while playing paintball should completely cover your skin. Although it is best to wear old clothes, avoid any with holes or rips that may expose your skin. Thicker clothes will provide a cushion against paintball impacts. If it is a cold day, you should wear heavy clothing, as paintball players commonly spend up to six hours outside.

While old clothing is usually the best choice, worn-out sneakers or boots may increase the risk of slipping and injuring yourself. You may want to purchase appropriate shoes to wear on the field. Plan for the terrain and conditions. If you will be playing in the woods, consider wearing boots with good ankle support to avoid sprains.

Make sure your goggles, mask, and helmet are designed for paintball. Never remove your goggles while on the playing field, even if they fog up, and never play with cracked or damaged goggles. Never fire your marker at someone who isn't wearing the proper equipment, especially goggles and a mask.

Other articles of protective clothing that you may want to consider include gloves, a hat, and neck protection—in other words, anything that will cover your skin. Some players also choose to wear chest and ankle protectors, knee and elbow pads, and cups (for male players).

Marker Safety

Before a regulation match, all markers are outfitted with a chronograph to measure paintball speed. Each marker is set to fire paintballs at a top speed of 300 feet (91.4 m) per second. Higher speeds could possibly damage safety gear and increase the potential for injuries and accidents. Because of the smaller playing area, indoor paintball facilities often set the top speed at 270 feet (82.3 m) per second.

When not on the field, players must engage the trigger safety on their markers or remove the air supply. This helps ensure that people won't accidentally get shot. In addition, players must have a barrel plug in the end of their markers. Engaging the safety and using a barrel plug make it

okay for players to remove goggles and other protective gear when they are off the field.

Take Care of Your Gear

Always take care of your equipment and make sure it works properly. You should never look down the barrel to see if it is loaded or jammed. Never try to fire anything but approved paintballs from your marker. When not on the playing field, keep a barrel plug in the end of your marker to avoid accidents. Never leave your marker or paintballs in the sun, as excessive heat can cause the gas inside CO_2 and NO_2 cartridges to expand and possibly explode. Remove the air cartridge from your marker when you are not using it.

Unless you are trained to repair air guns, you should never attempt to repair a broken marker. However, for routine maintenance, most experienced players like to clean their own markers. This allows the marker to keep firing smoothly. If you do your own maintenance, make sure you understand how to take a marker apart and put it back together again. There are books on the market and Web sites that provide step-by-step instructions on how to take apart, clean, and reassemble markers. You can find some of these resources in this book on pages 42–44.

The Future of Paintball

The first major paintball equipment supplier, Pursuit Marketing, Inc., sold between 7,000 and 8,000 markers in its first year of business. This was far more than the owners had ever hoped to sell. Most new businesses don't turn a profit for two or three years, but Pursuit Marketing began to make a profit

(*Facing page*) In the top photo, officials check a marker before a competition to measure the speed of the paintballs it shoots. In the bottom photo, you can see that the player has fitted his marker with a barrel plug for safety.

Making the Game Safer

In the pursuit to make paintball even safer than it already is, paintball manufacturers and governing bodies—such as the National Professional Paintball League (NPPL)—are constantly looking for ways to improve equipment and rules. In the years since the origin of paintball, key rule changes have helped to make it a remarkably safe activity. As with any sport, injuries are inevitable, but they can be reduced with relevant equipment and rule modifications.

Mandated safety changes that have occurred in professional paintball over the years include stronger goggles, the use of full face masks, and harsher punishment for breaking the rules. In 2005, the NPPL changed its official rulebook to include a twelve-game suspension for any player who sets a marker to fire more than one paintball per trigger pull. This rule is designed to make sure that no player has an unfair advantage and to make the game safer for everyone.

within six months of opening. It was obvious from the beginning that paintball was the new rage, and it has continued to grow by leaps and bounds ever since.

Each year, the Sports Goods and Manufacturers Association collects data regarding 100 popular American sports. Its report showed that 7,678,000 people had participated in paintball at least once during the year 2001. The same report, it is interesting to note, showed that of the 100 sports reviewed, paintball was the one that led to the fewest injuries. That means fewer people were injured playing paintball than participating in sports such as bowling and fishing. Since the 2001 report was issued, paintball has grown in popularity. In 2002, 8,679,000 Americans participated in paintball at least once. In 2003, 9,835,000 Americans played the sport.

Each year, thousands attend the Paintball Expo West in Pomona, California, to learn about the latest in paintball technology and merchandise. These paintball players are modeling some of the latest innovations in paintball gear.

New technology and playing styles guarantee that people will continue to flock to paintball. In 2003, paintball retailers made about $3.8 billion from the sale of paintball equipment worldwide. With numbers like these, it is obvious that paintball is a fast-growing sport. Now that you know the basics, you, too, can experience one of the most exciting and challenging games around.

GLOSSARY

aggressive Characterized by high energy, quick actions, and an urge to attack first.

agitate To cause something to move by shaking or prodding it.

biodegradable Capable of being broken down by microorganisms into elements that won't harm the environment.

bunker An obstruction behind which a paintball player can hide and shoot at other players.

camouflage Clothing or devices designed to conceal the user by imitating the colors and textures of the surroundings.

cartridge A small, sealed case used to load a substance into something, such as compressed air in a paintball marker.

chronograph An electronic device that measures the speed of a paintball as it leaves the barrel of a marker.

compress To squeeze.

disband To break up.

disposable Designed to be thrown away after use.

eject To remove a player from a competition for breaking the rules.

gelatin A plastic-like natural substance that is used to make paintball capsules.

inconspicuous Not easily seen or noticed.

projectile An object that can be thrown, fired, or launched.

propellant A compressed gas that can be used to launch an object, such as a paintball.

regulation Approved for use, or conforming to guidelines set up by an officially recognized governing body.

survivalist Someone who is determined to stay alive or stay in a game by relying on his or her instincts and knowledge of the surroundings.

suspension The temporary removal of a player from a team as punishment for breaking the rules.

terrain The general physical features of a piece of land.

water-soluble Capable of being washed away with water.

FOR MORE INFORMATION

Action Pursuit Games Magazine (subscriptions)
P.O. Box 68040
Anaheim, CA 92817
(800) 999-9718
Web site: http://www.actionpursuitgames.com

National Collegiate Paintball Association (NCPA)
530 E. South Avenue
Chippewa Falls, WI 54729
(612) 605-8323
Web site: http://www.college-paintball.com

National Professional Paintball League, Inc. (NPPL)
419 Main Street, Suite 402
Huntington Beach, CA 92648
(714) 536-9050
Web site: http://www.nppl.tv

National X Ball League (NXL)
6000 Kieran
St. Laurent, QC H4S 2B5
(514) 337-1779, ext. 229
Web site: http://www.nxlpaintball.com

Paintball 2 Xtremes Magazine (PB2X)
570 Mantua Boulevard
Sewell, NJ 08080
(888) 834-6026
Web site: http://www.pb2x.com

Paintball Magazine
4201 Vanowen Place
Burbank, CA 91505
(800) 877-5528
Web site: http://www.corin.com/pbmag

Web Sites

Due to the changing nature of Internet links, Rosen Publishing has developed an online list of Web sites related to the subject of this book. This site is updated regularly. Please use this link to access the list:

http://www.rosenlinks.com/scc/paint

FOR FURTHER READING

Braun, Jerry, et. al. *The Complete Guide to Paintball*, fourth edition (with DVD). Long Island City, NY: Hatherleigh Press, 2006.

Cooper, Guy D. *How to Operate a Safe Paintball Field*. Englewood, CO: Pro Star Sports, Inc., 2001.

Cooper, Guy D. *How to Run Your Own Paintball Tournament*. Englewood, CO: Pro Star Sports, Inc., 2003.

Elbe, Ronald E. *Paintball, the Wizard's Way: The Authoritative Book on Paintball Equipment, Strategy, and Tactics*. Chino Valley, AZ: Blacksmith, 1994.

Grubish, Don. *Scenario Paintball: Tips, Tools, and Tactics from the Trenches*. New Brighton, MN: Modern Press, 2005.

Sekely, Larry. *Paintball 101*. New Bern, NC: Trafford Publishing, 2005.

BIBLIOGRAPHY

Barnes, Bill. *Paintball! Strategies and Tactics*. Memphis, TN: Mustang Publishing, 1993.

BeaYoungs.com. "Paintball Newz." Retrieved February 7, 2006 (http://www.beayoungs.com/pbnewz.htm).

BrandBeat.com. "Sales of U.S. Recreational Products Push $70 Billion." SGMA International Press Release. June 29, 2004. Retrieved February 7, 2006 (http://www.brandbeat.com/brandbeat/?m=200406).

Braun, Jerry, et. al. *The Complete Guide to Paintball*. Long Island City, NY: Hatherleigh Press, 2003.

Daisy.com. "Daisy.com: History." Retrieved November 15, 2005 (http://www.daisy.com/history.html).

EnjoyTurkey.com. "Basic Rules of Paintball." Retrieved February 7, 2006 (http://www.enjoyturkey.com/Tours/Interest/Rules.htm).

EnjoyTurkey.com. "What Is Paintball?" Retrieved February 7, 2006 (http://www.enjoyturkey.com/Tours/Interest/Equipment.htm).

Khan, Sami. "Tips for Beginners." The Paintball Times. February 1993. Retrieved February 7, 2006 (http://www.paintballtimes.com/Article.asp?ID=9).

Kloehn, Paul. "What Is the History of Paintball?" World and Regional Paintball Information Guide. Retrieved February 7, 2006 (http://www.warpig.com/paintball/newbie/rspfaq.shtml#history).

Little, John R., and Curtis F. Wong, eds. *Ultimate Guide to Paintball*. Burbank, CA: CFW Enterprises, 2001.

National Professional Paintball League, Inc. "Official Rule Book–2005." March 1, 2005. Retrieved January 31, 2006 (http://www.nppl.tv/2005-Rules-final-3-1-05.pdf).

PaintballNexus.com. "Safety." December 24, 2004. Retrieved November 16, 2005 (http://www.paintballnexus.com/index.php?id=b_11_1103943086).

Sapp, Rick. *Paintball Digest*. Iola, WI: Krause Publications, 2004.

SGMA International Press Release. "Extreme Sports Are Still 'Hot' in the U.S." June 5, 2003. Retrieved February 7, 2006 (http://www.sgma.com/press/2003/press1054913159-22711.html).

WakeWorld.com. "Extreme Sports: They Have National Appeal." SGMA International Press Release. August 8, 2004. Retrieved February 7, 2006 (http://www.wakeworld.com/news/2004/sgma1.asp).

Warpig.com. "Ten Paintball Safety Tips." Retrieved November 16, 2005 (http://www.warpig.com/paintball/newbie/safety.shtml).

INDEX

About the Author

Greg Roza is a writer and editor specializing in library books and educational materials. He lives in Hamburg, New York, with his wife, Abigail, his daughter, Autumn, and his son, Lincoln. Roza has a master's degree in English from SUNY Fredonia, and he loves to stay in shape by participating in outdoor activities.

Photo Credits

Designer: Nelson Sá; **Editor:** Christopher Roberts
Photo Researcher: Amy Feinberg